Bank of
Merrill Lynch

D0594244

Wine Bar Theory is an attitude and an approach to work.

It saves you time.

It's not about cutting corners or doing things poorly. It's not about sloping off early before the job is done.

It's about wanting the very best and not settling for less.

It's a theory that can pave your road to success.

Φ

Whether people work in an office, a school or a hospital, a tennis club or a scuba-diving shop, they always find ways of working, individually and together, to get the job done.

Most people end up working very hard, and long hours. They think these are good signs. If they are working hard and round the clock it must mean they are doing a good job.

Not necessarily.

Busy is not the same as effective. Lots of people are busy, but very busy people don't always achieve lots. People at work often run a marathon to move their organization forward by a step.

There are many reasons why this might happen. It's not usually because they are stupid, wilful or lazy.

It can be because their roles are confused or the priorities aren't clear. It can be because they believe they have to do things a certain way and it can never change. It can be because no one can make a decision.

Or because everyone is so busy doing urgent things they never get round to what's important.

Wine Bar Theory is the antidote to all that.

Following the 28 Wine Bar Theory rules will help you do an excellent job, without stress and without needing huge amounts of time.

The rules will apply to the organization you already work in or a new one you want to start.

They will help you succeed personally, whether you are the boss or the doorman.

They will give you the licence to challenge and change things that take hours to complete but don't really take your business forward much at all. You could be using that time so much better!

Wine Bar Theory wins you time.

It helps you see things you can do more easily and things you don't need to do at all. The time and energy you save you can use to do something else instead.

You might spend it at work learning new stuff, or taking time out to think and to imagine. Or outside it, recharging your batteries, or just having fun.

Maybe you could play ball, knit a sweater, go fish.

Or if you're like me, go to a wine bar and relax with friends!

Of course, if you work somewhere where people don't make any difference to what goes on and marvellous things just jump out of a box by magic then this is not a book for you.

Put it down now and go find yourself another book!

Sorry, wait a moment.

If you work somewhere where things jump out of a box by magic, you will need something to do while you are guarding the box.

So read this book anyway. It will tell you what the rest of us are doing while you are sitting there.

OK. Let's go. Here are the rules.

The Rules

1. **Make your business sustainable**
2. **Keep it simple**
3. **Keep asking**
4. **Reason to believe**
5. **Get a distinction**
6. **Know where you are going**
7. **Aim to do more, not the same**
8. **Don't increase profit at the expense of growth**
9. **Enrich your customer**
10. **Cut smart**
11. **Invest in winning marketing**
12. **Don't guess ...**
13. **... and don't invite guesses**
14. **Be more responsible: give away responsibility**

①

Make your business sustainable

Now, before you start thinking about wind farms, climate change and the future of the planet, I don't mean that. That's a recent kidnapping of the word 'sustainable', which was around doing a perfectly good job for years before anyone thought of installing a solar panel or growing themselves a turf roof.

Let's set 'sustainable' free again. It simply means 'can keep going'.

People who run businesses are often encouraged by people who don't (usually called advisers) to write lots of documents and presentations about the strategic vision and mission of their business.

This is great for the advisers because it gives them something to talk about, for months, sometimes years. Because advisers want to be sustainable too they tend to prolong this as long as they can, and create wealth for themselves while they do.

"Without continual growth and progress, such words as improvement, achievement and success have no meaning."

BENJAMIN FRANKLIN (1706–90)
PHILOSOPHER, INVENTOR,
WRITER AND DIPLOMAT

Trouble is, it's usually a waste of time for the business they are advising.

Every business can come up with its mission in one minute, and write it on a piece of paper you could stick on a fridge.

Here, for example, is a mission statement for a business that makes cakes:

'We make cakes. We want to keep going.'

OK, just to be clear, that only works as a mission statement if you are a cake business. Using those exact words would worry people if you were a mountain guide business.

To write the mission statement for the business you work in, tune the first sentence a bit to make it say what you do. The second sentence should work just fine, whatever business you are. Leave it be. 'We want to keep going.'

Then tell the advisers they can go and keep going, too.

Hooray! You've already saved some time and money.

Now you're in business. Simple.

Keep it simple

The world is full of over-educated nitwits, who devote their lives to making things complicated.

Here's why complicated is not good.

Complicated is hard to understand. If a business is complicated, most people don't get what it does so they find it hard to join in or help.

They also run away because it makes them feel stupid.

If you think something is complicated it's because you haven't finished thinking about it. If you haven't finished thinking about it that means you don't quite get it. If you don't understand something properly, you will find it impossible to explain it to anyone else.

Don't assume people understand complicated things. They don't. Work it through. Don't pass on complex messages. Distil the significant.

Smart people make the complicated simple.

Make sure you can describe your business simply. Then you can explain it to someone attractive you just met and are sitting next to at a dinner party, or on a park bench.

By the time you finish telling them what you do they need to be looking deeply into your eyes. Not lying face down in their soup. Or wandering off to find another bench.

Go on then!

You have thirty seconds. Captivate them!

Once you can tell another person what your business is and why it's special, without their eyes glazing over, you are on the road to success.

You will be able to ask them to come help you do it or to buy some of what it is you are already fetching or making.

So how do you keep it simple?

By asking simple questions.

That's the third rule of Wine Bar Theory.

Keep asking

Here's a simple question: Why?

Here's another one: What if?

People and businesses stay fresh by questioning assumptions. Especially their own.

The longer someone spends doing the same thing, the harder questioning it can become. Because they've invested so much time building up their own conviction they don't want to knock it down.

So for some people it becomes harder to say, 'Do you know what? I don't know.' They feel they already know all the answers, or they ought to. They stop asking the questions. They say things like this:

'She will never agree to that.'

'That failed years ago.'

'That's embarrassing.'

'Don't even go there.'

People locked up in that phase need release. They need to go somewhere where they can be free to ask simple questions again.

The more time you spend asking simple questions, the smarter those questions become.

Here are the sort of questions people in a smart business ask:

'Do we have to do that every day?'

'Why do three people need to sign it?'

'Does anyone actually use this?'

The answers often aren't so obvious.

A business that follows Wine Bar Theory knows that 'I don't know' can be a really good answer, as long as it's followed by 'let's find out'.

A long time ago I asked a hugely successful global commodity dealer if he'd mind if I asked him an indiscreet question about his business.

This is what he replied: 'There are no indiscreet questions. There are only indiscreet answers.'

A smart business keeps asking indiscreet questions of itself.

Reason to believe

If you're thinking of starting up a new business that might be sustainable, and meet Wine Bar Theory Rule 1, be sure to apply the second and third rules too. Keep it simple and keep asking.

If what you are planning to start doing seems complicated, and you don't know whether it will work or not, that's because you haven't finished thinking about it.

So don't do it. At least not yet.

It might turn out to be successful if you just go ahead with it anyway, but you can't be sure. That's hope, not belief. It relies on luck, not judgement.

If you like betting on hope and luck, buy yourself a lottery ticket and take the day off.

Take the dog to the park and think some more about your plan.

You need to move it from hope to belief. You get there by asking simple questions about what you plan to start fetching or making.

Belief and judgement can prove to be wrong, of course, but they are wrong much less often than hope and luck are.

What questions should you ask? Here are your ten for starters.

1. Who needs this?

2. How do they meet that need now?

3. Why would they buy this instead?

4. How many people could buy it?

5. How would I reach them?

6. How many of them will buy it?

7. How much would they pay for it?

8. How often will they buy it?

9. How much will it cost to fetch or make each one?

10. How many people will I need to do that?

Take your time in the park to answer those questions. Judge your answers carefully. In particular, the difference between how many people *could* buy something and how many *will* is almost always huge.

The answers will produce a business plan for you. They will show you what has to happen for your idea to be a success: for it to bring in more money than it costs you to do it.

When you have that plan, ask yourself one more question.

Do you believe it?

Now you know whether to do it or not, which leads us on to the fifth rule of Wine Bar Theory.

Don't worry, it's not as frightening as it sounds.

"Why, sometimes I've believed as many as six impossible things before breakfast."

LEWIS CARROLL (1832–98)
AUTHOR OF *ALICE'S ADVENTURES IN WONDERLAND*

Get a distinction

A central bank economist who became
a headmistress once told me something very
smart, and it was not at all economic. This is
what she said:

'When you pick a school for your child, remember
no child should be in the bottom 25 per cent of
the class.'

Excuse me?

What she meant was, don't put your child in
a school where he or she will be consistently
outshone. Choose somewhere he or she can
consistently shine.

It's the same with business.

Don't be an also-ran. Don't be in the bottom
25 per cent of a class. Find something you can
do better than others.

For your business to be sustainably successful
it must stand out from others. If you do the same
thing as others they, not you, will determine what

"Conformity is the jailer of freedom and the enemy of growth."

JOHN F. KENNEDY (1917–63)
35TH PRESIDENT OF THE UNITED STATES

you can achieve. If people can more easily get what you are fetching or making from someone else, then that's exactly what they will do.

Businesses that do the same thing as others often try to make themselves stand out by charging less. But that difference doesn't last. Because the competition quickly follows them down in price.

You need to be able to do something important which others can't easily follow or copy. That distinction can be in the product itself, or in the way you serve it up to your customers.

It's called value. It's a beautiful word.

Make what you do unique in a way customers will value. Then you can charge a price that reflects how much they appreciate the difference. The less distinctive you are, the more your prices and opportunities will be determined by others.

Get as far away as you can from others doing the same or similar things, and you can set your own prices. Just don't overestimate how much people appreciate uniqueness. They'll make do with a 'good enough' alternative if it's much cheaper.

So don't be the same. Be special.

As well as knowing what it does, a brilliant business also knows what it wants to become.

Know where you are going

To do that, first find your dream.

What do you imagine your business could become one day? What might it look like?

Draw a picture of that.

Compare that picture with where you are today.

Now, colour in the road between the two.

How long will it take to get there, what needs to happen and by when for you to reach that goal?

Once you've answered those questions you have a simple map to your future and you will recognize things that take you off course for what they are.

Diversions.

If you don't know where you are going, everywhere seems like an intriguing option.

When everywhere is an option, you may not like where you end up.

Wandering off course is exhausting, too.

Don't forget, Wine Bar Theory is about winning time, not wasting it.

Businesses which are clear on their direction know their priorities. They don't exhaust themselves doing things that take them backwards or off to the side. They know what progress is.

Brilliant businesses travel, poor ones ramble.

Always carry your map.

Aim to do more,
not the same

There are only three states that things can be in: moving forward, standing still, or going backwards.

Standing still is really quite hard for a business because everything around it is usually moving fast. People's needs and tastes change, new ways of doing things get invented and new businesses arrive to compete for customers.

It's a dynamic world.

So while there is nothing wrong with standing still, it is a hard thing to do and dangerous to aim for.

If you aim to stand still when things are moving all around you, you will go backwards.

Going backwards in business is not a good thing. Going backwards, conceding ground, becoming less important to people – these are all warning signs the business may not be able to keep going.

That's why businesses like growth. It means they are moving forwards, gaining ground and becoming a bit more important. That gives them more chance of being a sustainable, successful and lasting business.

Growing businesses can do nice things: throw parties; say 'well done' to everyone. Maybe even pay a bonus. Or take everyone to the wine bar to celebrate their success.

They can create opportunities for people to go places, achieve things and have fun all the while.

Happy, engaged people who feel like they are working in the right place where there are opportunities start to feel like they own the joint, and that encourages them to look after it rather than abuse it.

That includes having ideas for things the business can do better and more of. They help it grow more.

Smart people want to work for businesses like that.

That's another reason why growth is a good thing.

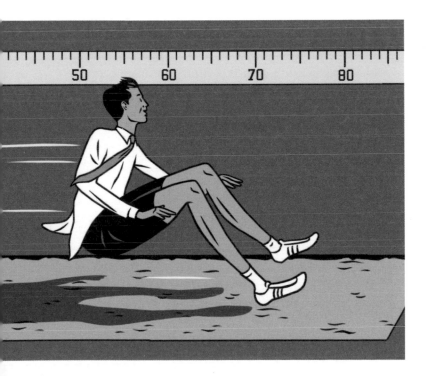

Don't increase profit at the expense of growth

Hey, wait a minute! Let's not get ahead of ourselves. What is growth anyway?

Growth is selling more of what you are fetching or making. Growth is about bringing in more revenue (money from sales). That's not the same as making more profit (revenue minus costs), though the two can go together.

Doing more + selling more = growth

There are two ways to grow revenues: sell more of what you make or fetch at the same or lower prices, or put your prices up without losing too many customers as a result.

Businesses that have more revenue than they did this time last year are growing. Businesses that have more profit than they made last year may not be. They may just be reducing costs.

Businesses with less revenue are going backwards, even if it takes a while for them to realize it.

Unless the reason they have less revenue is because they decided to concentrate on fewer things they do really well and stop some things they don't, of course.

Growing revenues will increase profit too as long as you aren't increasing costs at the same or a faster rate.

Many businesses are so focused on profit that they don't spend much time paying attention to revenue. Often they increase profits for a time by cutting costs at every opportunity. They think that is clever.

It isn't. You can't keep cutting costs because if you do, you eventually fall over.

A business that thinks it can cut its way to success will never be sustainable – it will break the first rule of Wine Bar Theory.

You can't keep going by cutting costs because in the end you run out of costs to cut.

Success is growing profitable revenue.

Enrich your customer

Businesses keep growing by providing things that customers value more than the money they have to pay for them, and the time they have to give up to use them. Customers buy them willingly because they feel enriched by them.

When people find enriching things they need or want, they keep on buying them and they tell their friends and family about them, too.

Products that keep on selling enrich the people who buy them as well as the business that makes them.

Sustainable happiness!

How do you get to that happy place and stay there?

By making sure you know why people buy from you and exactly what they do with your product once they have bought it.

And by taking nothing for granted.

Don't assume your customers are all the same, or that they all value the same things in what you do.

Different people appreciate different things.

Wine Bar Theory businesses take the time to find out and understand these differences. When they do, they make sure they keep doing all the things their customers value.

They also make sure they aren't wasting time doing things no one notices or worries about.

Caring about what customers really value leads us sharply on to the next rule.

Cut smart

Wine Bar Theory businesses want all the work they do to go towards creating things their customers value.

They cut the stuff the customer doesn't care about and wouldn't pay for, saving time and effort too.

Costs in a business are there to help it drive revenue. They should relate to the things your customers like about what you do.

If you cut costs indiscriminately you will end up with less revenue over time. Because the chances are customers won't like what you do as much as they used to.

There is only one way to reduce costs sensibly and it's never by cutting a certain percentage of everything. It's by examining everything you do in real detail and checking two things:

Do you still need to do it all?

Could the things you still need to do be done better?

Businesses tend to keep doing things they've always done, and progressively add to them each time they think of something else they could do as well.

That way they get progressively busier but no wiser. As they get busier they become less clear what really matters; less sure what customers really value in what they do.

Wine Bar Theory businesses don't mistake busy for effective.

Smart businesses regularly re-examine each element of what they do, and ask whether the customer really needs and values the work they are doing. If the customer doesn't value it much or even notice it, it may not be necessary to do it at all.

Often businesses forget to check that and they end up working for themselves, rather than their customers. Why? Because they have always done things that way. They end up doing things they don't really need to do, and incurring unnecessary costs.

Smart costs are different. They are not the enemy of profit, they are the friend of revenue.

Let's meet a smart cost now. It's revenue's very best friend.

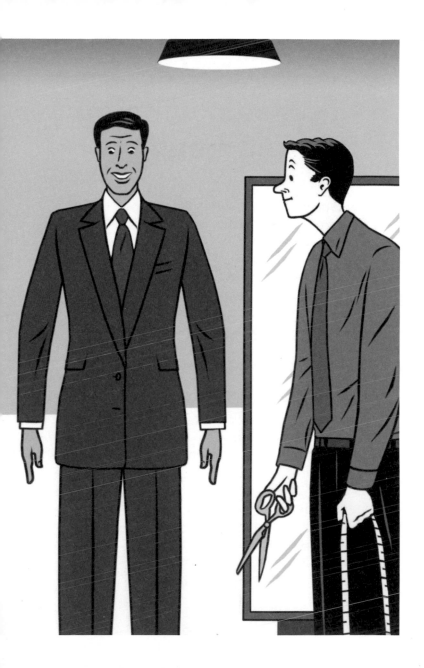

(11)

Invest in winning marketing

Business people are often suspicious of marketing. Or scared of it. Brilliant business people are not.

Marketing encourages others to buy what you fetch or make. It costs money to do it. Of course. But done well it costs less to do than the money your customers give you as a result of it.

What's not to like about that?

People who are suspicious of marketing aren't quite sure what it is or how to do it. They know they are supposed to do it but they don't like it because they see it as a cost.

They think of a cost as something that reduces wealth. They wonder if they could get away with doing less or none of it, because then they would make more profit and be wealthier.

This is why that is not smart.

"The formula 'two and two make five' is not without its attractions."

FYODOR DOSTOYEVSKY (1821–81)
NOVELIST AND ESSAYIST

If you go into a bar and meet a man who says: 'For every $5 you give me I will give you $10 back', how many $5 bills do you have? Answer? As many as you can lay your hands on until he stops giving you more in exchange for them.

Many businesses have a fixed budget for marketing. If they met a $10-for-$5 man in the bar they'd say: 'Great. But I only have three $5 bills available to spend.'

Wine Bar Theory is about making sure the things you do at work produce real benefit.

Smart marketing makes you more money than it costs. It adds to your wealth. It does not subtract from it.

Something that makes you more money than it costs to do is something you should do more of. Not less. Or none.

Smart marketing might be an offer you send out to people, a customer reception you hold, an event you attend or a promotion you stage. If it costs you less to do than you make as a result, do it again, and then again. If it loses you money, change it.

So when marketing finds you a $10-for-$5 opportunity, keep investing in it while you are winning, until you stop winning.

Don't guess ...

Smart marketing is about asking the right questions to find winning formulas.

Smart marketers carefully gather evidence, interpret it and then act on it.

Smart marketers offer people choices between things they understand and measure their responses. They try out different controlled approaches to see what people like and prefer.

Do people choose a gift or a discount?

Do they respond to a better price offer for buying more?

Does paying in instalments make a difference?

How many prefer blue to green?

Marketing should ask questions of persuaded people (your customers) and unpersuaded people (people who could become your customers) and measure their answers.

"The strongest principle of growth lies in human choice."

GEORGE ELIOT (1819–80)
NOVELIST

The responses to different approaches will show you what is more or less successful.

Things that are successful need to be repeated until they aren't successful any more.

Things that aren't successful need to be stopped and re-thought.

If you can't measure whether something is successful or not, don't do it.

Smart marketing asks, tests and measures.

It finds you winning $10-for-$5 formulas and lets you take advantage of them for as long as they last.

While they do, you should be marketing more and looking for new opportunities like them.

There's one more crucial thing to understand about marketing questions though.

It's the next rule.

(13)

... and don't invite guesses

Smart marketing questions aim to establish how people will behave when they are presented with choices between alternatives they know or can picture.

They don't ask people for opinions about things they don't know or understand.

If you ask someone for their opinion on something they haven't seen or can't imagine they will give you a random answer.

How would you like a telephone you can carry in your pocket all the time?

If you'd asked people that question in 1990 most people would have said 'no, thanks' and probably thought you were a bit weird to be asking. Today everyone says 'yes'.

You can't rely on the answers people give to marketing questions to tell you whether a new product will succeed.

"If I'd asked people what they wanted they would have said faster horses."

HENRY FORD (1863–1947)
FOUNDER OF THE FORD MOTOR COMPANY

They don't know because they haven't seen it yet. So you can't trust their response, good or bad.

To launch something new, as Wine Bar Theory Rules 4 and 5 say, you need to have your own well-founded reasons to believe in it.

That's business.

The next rule is an essential feature of any brilliant business.

It sounds like it can't be true but believe me it is.

(14)

Be more responsible: give away responsibility

When you are growing up, your parents and your teachers tell you what to do.

That's a good idea because when you are growing up you haven't found out whether sticking your head in the fire is a good plan or not. You also don't know your multiplication tables, so having someone make you learn them is better than going your own way and not learning them.

Adult–child, teacher–pupil relationships are very good for young learners. They are not good for grown-up businesses that want to grow more.

People in business need to be responsible. Unless you want them to behave like children, that is.

People need to be given responsibility for things and encouraged to take on more when they can.

They want to be told the rules and given support. They don't want their job done for them.

The people in business best placed to make decisions are the people closest to the actual work. That applies as much to the doorman as it does to the big boss.

The best person to take decisions about the opening and closing of the door, letting people in and showing them out, is the person in charge of the door.

If the boss wants to take those decisions, he/she had better be ready to be on the door all the time.

Since there are plenty of other jobs in the business as well as the door handling, that's going to be tough.

Any boss that tries to do that is running two bad things at the same time: a business that can't grow, and the risk of a heart attack. Also, they can never go on holiday. Or visit a wine bar.

Bosses like that think they are indispensable. The graveyard is piled high with them. While they're alive they can never rest.

Except they can rest assured of one thing. No one will ever do anything without asking them first or deviate from what they think were their instructions.

"Look for people who will aim for the remarkable, who will not settle for the routine."

DAVID OGILVY (1911–99)
ADVERTISING EXECUTIVE

So the boss had better be sure they thought of everything when they told them what to do.

That boss also makes it clear that initiative and ideas are not welcome. So anyone who has either of them offers none, or leaves.

Since we know people with ideas grow businesses, that's a problem.

Don't let it happen. There is no need. The responsibility you delegate you never actually lose. You just make others responsible for it too.

Then you can reward them for how well they look after it. They will usually do it well because it's theirs and they have several reasons to care and nurture it. People spend their own money better than they spend other people's.

Businesses where everyone feels responsible don't blame people if someone makes a mistake. They set about fixing the problem and learning from what happened.

A business that doesn't blame doesn't fear. Businesses without fear do brave things. In Wine Bar Theory businesses people aren't afraid of responsibility.

That moves us boldly on to a question: what type of decisions do responsible, brave people take?

Be brave,
not reckless

Brave does not mean reckless. Bravery is the assessment and acceptance of risk.

A reckless person crosses the road without looking. A fearful person doesn't cross the road. A brave person reads the traffic and crosses when it's safe.

Smart businesses marshal evidence and take brave decisions on the back of it.

What's the worst that can happen?

The worst that can happen is not that a business goes the wrong way and makes a mistake. You can correct a mistake when you spot it.

The worst that can happen is a business doesn't make decisions on where to go and what to do. It doesn't go anywhere and it does nothing.

Those businesses stop in their tracks and start going backwards. Smart people leave them.

"Life shrinks
or expands
in proportion
to one's
courage."

ANAÏS NIN (1903–77)
WRITER

Smart drivers know mirror, indicate, brake.

Smart businesses know look, consider, act.

Smart businesses make informed decisions
to accept risk. Because they understand that
if you don't risk anything you risk a lot more.

To capture future opportunity, business people
have to imagine what might be possible and be
brave enough to build it.

They have to believe: in people and ideas.

⑯

Be better at standing things up

Wine Bar Theory businesses know that to create their future they need to nurture and develop ideas.

Many businesses are beset with analysts who tell them the future can be found by reviewing the numbers of the past. They pore over historical outcomes and figures and use them for predictions. They project the past forward. They know nothing about the future.

The trouble with figures of the past is they can't show you what might have been. They don't show you the revenue the business could have had if it had done more or done things differently. They don't show you your lost opportunity.

A business's lost opportunity can be bigger than the business itself.

People who rely on analyzing the past are good at telling you why something won't work. They are experts at knocking down ideas.

Smart businesses know that you need to take calculated risks. They're brave, not reckless. They experiment, accepting some things will fail.

They correct error quickly and don't make the same mistake twice.

Once they find the basis for a decision, they make it. They back their belief in a new future, not a continuation of the past.

They stand things up.

Once businesses get that it's smart to back responsible, brave people, it makes them realize something about the sort of people they need to hire.

"Trust the dots will somehow connect in your future ... trust in your gut, destiny, life, karma, whatever."

STEVE JOBS (1955–2011)
ENTREPRENEUR AND CO-FOUNDER
OF APPLE

(17)

Insist on the best

To keep on growing, a smart business has to delegate responsibility to its people to multiply its energy and its speed, and to keep it in touch with what's really going on.

Unless superheroes work there of course, in which case everyone else can sit back and leave them to it. They can just marvel at their wondrous powers.

That's pretty rare. Most businesses have to get by without superheroes.

Once they recognize all the superheroes must be working somewhere else, smart managers put a big premium on hiring smart people.

Defensive managers who want to hide their own inadequacies never hire anyone who is as good as or better than them.

They hire people who are smaller than the job they are brought in to do, who they think will not be a threat to their position.

"I'm easily satisfied with the very best."

WINSTON CHURCHILL (1874–1965)
BRITISH PRIME MINISTER

Smart managers respond to their own inadequacies by hiring people who are as good as they are, or better. That way they bring in people who are bigger than the job.

Big people expand businesses.

From their first day those people look to improve the business and expand their role. They take responsibility. That's a vital ingredient of business growth.

So never say, 'She was brilliant but I don't think she would have been satisfied with the job, so I offered it to someone else instead.'

If you ever do that you are reducing the strength of the business you are working in, not increasing it. That's the opposite of helpful.

Insist on the best talent and when you see it, seize it. Those are the people who take initiative and help you achieve. Don't ever let them go.

Smart people recruit their successor because smart people want to get on.

But wait!

It's not just about getting good people. It's how you play them together.

Surround yourself with specialist excellence

A brilliant business is a brilliant team.

Teams are made up of people who do different jobs towards one goal.

If you are trying to build a brilliant business, be wary of generalists when you pick new people to join it.

Generalists are quite good at several things. Specialists are very good at something.

A team made up of people who are quite good at several things will always lose to a team of people who are very good at what they individually do, all playing in their special position, understanding the part they play in the overall success.

Ask someone you are thinking of hiring, 'What are you truly excellent at?' Have them show you the evidence. If you are convinced by it and you need that special excellence in your team, hire it.

Build your team on excellence in every function. Never compromise on quite good, unless that's what you aspire to be.

Once in a blue moon you may stumble across a genuine polymath: someone who is very good at everything. They can play in almost any position in your team.

Be happy. You have done very well. They are hard to find.

Don't be tempted to spend your life looking for them though. There aren't enough hours in the day. Target instead people who are excellent at one (or two) things and play to their strengths.

Smart businesses, like smart people, are truly excellent at very few things. Knowing what those things are – and majoring in them – is a key to business success.

If a business thinks it's really good at everything, it's kidding itself. Don't worry though, it won't be kidding anyone else.

It's wonderful when you find excellent people to bring into your team, but the work doesn't stop there of course.

If talent exists, promote it

I once bought a business from a smart man for $225 million. He and his wife had built it up from nothing. They had a simple philosophy for hiring people. This was it:

Always recruit the tea boy.

Whenever they needed to bring someone in, they always tried to hire at the lowest point in the organization and move everyone else up.

They kept all their best people.

Often businesses think geniuses only live outside. So they like to hire externally. They find that reassuring.

Those businesses tend to be highly impressed by people in interviews. They admire what people say more than what they do.

They either don't consider the internal candidate or they like to say, 'he's good, but he's not ready'.

Businesses that like to bring people in from outside to fill big jobs send one of two excluding messages to the people they already have. Either 'yes, we considered you and we decided you weren't up to it,' or 'no, we didn't consider you'.

Wine Bar Theory businesses know their own people and make them more ready every day to do the next job.

Sometimes, of course, there's a pure skill requirement that you just have to bring in from outside because it doesn't exist within the business.

That ought to be the exception not the rule for all but the smallest business, but if you decide you have to bring in a senior recruit, read the next rule before you do.

"Mediocrity knows nothing higher than itself, but talent instantly recognizes genius."

SIR ARTHUR CONAN DOYLE (1859–1930)
PHYSICIAN AND WRITER

Beware the Plausible Idiot

Nine times out of ten when you promote someone who you already know is talented and effective it works out well for the business and for them.

If even half the senior people you decide to bring in from outside turn out to be any good then you are doing quite well.

That's because you will often hire a Plausible Idiot.

It's easy to do because there are a lot of them about and they seem great when you meet them.

You fall for a Plausible Idiot in an interview because you forget to ask for evidence of their success. They've never had any.

Well, hardly any. Remember, even a stopped clock will be right twice a day.

Plausible Idiots are just about the most dangerous people you can hire – they are much

"The most fluent talkers or most plausible reasoners are not always the justest thinkers."

WILLIAM HAZLITT (1778–1830)
WRITER

worse than people who are limited in what
they can do.

Damage caused by Plausible Idiots knows no
limits. They persuade people black is white.
They explain it's ten to three when it's five
past four.

They over-think. Faced with two doors, one marked
'Certain Death' and the other 'Everlasting Joy', they
choose the first one because they suspect a trick.

They are eloquent and convincing. Just wrong.

If you find yourself with a Plausible Idiot in your
business, get them out without delay.

Smart, proven people will grow into bigger
jobs. The business knows what it needs to do
to help them.

People who come in from outside are often
deemed to be geniuses from another galaxy.
The business sits back and waits for their
supernatural excellence to appear. If it doesn't,
it can take a year for everyone to realize.

The best you can hope for when that happens is
that your business has stood still. More often it
will have gone backwards. It will have lost three
precious things: ground, momentum and time.

Most likely it will be worse than that. Plausible Idiots repel good people and attract people like themselves. There's only one type of person who will work for more than a very short time for a Plausible Idiot. And that's another one.

The longer you let them stay the more you will have to repair.

So take great care when you hire. In truth, geniuses rarely come and knock on your door. They don't go out much. They tend to be well recognized where they are. And they're usually glued to the floor.

Before you bring in a senior recruit from outside, be sure they bring something new and better than what you have.

Once you have the right people in the business, the next job is to make sure you have the right number of them.

Not too many, not too few.

Do the job with the right resources, quickly

Wine Bar Theory managers recognize that the fewer, better people they have in their team the more effective they are likely to be, and the greater rewards and congratulations they will win themselves as the head of such a splendid, efficient outfit.

That means hiring inadequate people is a hugely expensive choice, even though they are usually paid less and seem cheaper.

What looks cheap often isn't really. What looks expensive often isn't either.

When it comes to people, it's almost always better to have fewer and strong than more and weak.

One day of one competent person is worth much more than two days of two people who aren't.

Competent people do things quickly and well. Competence wins you time. That's why it's better to let smart people work part time rather than lose them.

Work flexibly to get smart people. They are precious. Go the extra mile.

Wine Bar Theory business people reject inefficient, laborious processes. They don't want to be exhausted on Friday evening and need to sleep through the weekend so they've recovered in time to start again Monday. The very idea offends them.

It's surprising how many people want to feel exhausted so they know they are doing a good job.

Exhausted means inadequate resources are carrying out inefficient processes.

People justify inadequate resources by suggesting they save money.

Not if they cost you revenue they don't.

Consider this: If a hole needs digging and it takes three days to do it you have a choice about how to go about it.

You can have one man take three days to dig it or three men can do it in one day. The second is faster. The cost is the same.

"**Gentleness doesn't get work done, unless you happen to be a hen laying eggs.**"

COCO CHANEL (1883–1971)
FASHION DESIGNER

Aspire to create a business full of challengers. People who can think and want to improve. People who want the job done sooner and better. People who will reinvent you.

Keep questioning whether you have the right number of challengers. Smart people usually pay for themselves by helping bring in more revenue than they cost.

Celebrate winning time to spend in the wine bar, don't begrudge it.

So now we have the right number of the right people. Hurrah! At last. The job's done.

Actually, not quite.

There's one other area we haven't yet touched on but we must because it calls for smart thinking almost more than any other: acquiring another business.

It's a great way to grow if you get it right.

It's a terrible way to go if you don't.

Buyer beware

Here's the most important and the first question businesses should ask before they even think about acquiring another business:

Are we running our own business properly?

Sometimes an acquisition can make a good business better. Because it helps the acquiring business to do more of what it is already good at, and gives it some new ideas.

But if your own business needs fixing, buying another one won't solve it.

Fix it first and make the foundation on which to build firm.

To make an acquisition successful you have to be able to add something to the target company. If not, you will simply pay a great deal for what the target business has done in the past. And build yourself problems for the future.

To test that, ask these three questions about the business you think you might want to buy:

Is it growing already?

Can we help it grow more?

Can it help us grow more?

You are looking for a 'yes' three times.

If the combination doesn't help both the existing business and the acquired one, the likelihood is the acquired business won't even repeat what it did in the past but will go backwards.

A new acquisition is like a new toy. Everyone wants to go play with it.

They often abandon the old toys while they do.

That can mean the whole business – the old bit and the new bit – starts to go backwards.

To avoid this you need a smart welcome that dedicates good people full-time to bringing the businesses together. They can find new ways to raise revenues and make sure you aren't doing things twice. Without taking everyone's eye off what they did successfully before.

Before you go ahead, think how both sets of customers will benefit. Remember they are the people you are meant to be looking after most of all. Don't forget them – even for a second – or they'll quickly forget about you.

If you can't think why the two sets of customers would be pleased about your wonderful acquisition, you may need to think again...

Congratulations!

Your acquisition must have passed all those tests because you went through with it.

You're a big business now.

Next question: Has it made you stronger or weaker?

Answer: It depends on the next rule.

Think big, keep nimble

Why do so many acquisitions fail?

Because sometimes the disadvantages of a big organization outweigh its advantages.

Here's a list of the sort of things people say in a big company when they are experiencing disadvantages:

'Nothing I do makes any real difference.'

'They don't do things that way here.'

'Fill out this form.'

'I wouldn't know who to speak to about that.'

'The company goal is 5 per cent profit increase.'

Now here are some of the things people say in a big business when they are actually benefitting from its scale:

'They really put resources behind ideas.'

'I can build a career here.'

'I am being well trained.'

'I can always find expertise in-house.'

'This feels like a big, strong place.'

If it wants to hear the second list, not the first, a big business has to use its great resources to train and develop its people, and be prepared to back them and their ideas. It has to make them responsible for decisions.

Many big businesses don't do that, so they become big and ugly and no one loves them. The people who work in them think they can't change or influence anything and that makes them feel small, powerless and slow.

Successful small companies do the opposite and make their people feel big, powerful and quick.

Their people say things like this:

'We all get involved.'

'We are passionate about our product.'

'We want to delight our customers.'

"Bureaucracy is the death of all sound work."

ALBERT EINSTEIN (1849–1955)
THEORETICAL PHYSICIST

'We pride ourselves on fast response.'

'We know small details are what count.'

Notice they speak in the first person plural. They don't stand on ceremony. They don't wait to be asked. They pick up ringing phones when they aren't their own. They feel responsible. For themselves, for their team and for their business.

Successful small businesses are nimble. They have to be, so that they can stand out and compete against bigger businesses who have lots more people and money than them.

Remember the fifth rule? Small businesses know they need a distinction.

That's why so many big businesses ruin small businesses when they buy them. They don't recognize what attracted them to the small business in the first place and they smother it. Either through neglect or arrogance.

Small can be beautiful, big can be ugly. To be both big and beautiful, large businesses need to behave like small businesses but bring their advantages of resources and scale to bear too. If they manage to do that they can rule the world.

Big or small, if you want to succeed you have to make your business an inspiring place to work.

Lead more, manage less

In Wine Bar Theory businesses, attitude and atmosphere are set by people who are leaders. Not by people who are just about managing.

Some people think being a manager means you aren't allowed to be a human being as well. You have to stop being one when you come through the office door and you can't start being one again until you are on the bus home.

They think they have to assert authority when they are at work.

In asserting authority they forget all the things in life that makes any of us good at motivating and influencing others.

If you don't take an interest in people and empathize with them, you end up with few friends, no one to go to the wine bar with and no Christmas cards on your mantelpiece except the ones from your family (and they only send them because they have to).

Many managers think taking an interest and empathizing with someone undermines their authority. People earn respect from who they are and what they do, not by demanding it.

Here's the big secret of smart managing.

Good bosses aren't bossy.

Managers are allowed to be human beings.

They show that they are by regularly doing the jobs they ask others to do. And helping the rest of the time.

Here's another secret.

People in brilliant businesses talk to one another. Not once a year, awkwardly, in some formal appraisal room, but every day.

How are you getting on with that? Here's how we are doing so far. You don't find that so easy? Let's go through it again.

Leaders are managers who show the way. They support people to perform.

That's how smart business absorbs pressure, too. By sharing burdens.

Leaders also invite and answer questions.

There should be no question about the business that a leader is not prepared to answer.

Of course, that doesn't mean giving away secret recipes or putting things at risk by talking about them before they are ready.

It's the day-to-day business that should be talked about openly. If you are the boss and you won't tell your colleagues what's going on, then what is going on?

Don't expect people to feel responsible or take responsibility if they feel excluded.

Here's how smart leaders turn 'I' into 'we':

Inspiration, Ideas, Innovation, Improvement Implementation.

Wine Bar Theory leaders create inspiring places where people are encouraged to have ideas, to innovate and to change things to make them better. They implement those ideas, celebrate and then ask for more.

They encourage their people to be restless. To challenge and suggest. To ask the simple questions. To bring about positive change.

Here's the other big thing smart leaders do.

"It is better
to lead from
behind and
to put others
in front,
especially when
you celebrate
victory."

NELSON MANDELA (1918–)
FORMER SOUTH AFRICAN PRESIDENT
AND NOBEL LAUREATE

Recognize real success

There are three things that influence what we think about a job:

What we have to do.

How much we get paid for it.

Who we have to work for.

People can compromise over the first two. The third one they can't.

It might not be the most exciting job, and perhaps you can manage with mediocre pay. But you can't live with a fool for a boss. Life is too short.

A foolish boss doesn't recognize one basic need.

It's what makes people want to achieve and keep achieving. This is what it is called.

Recognition.

To give it, a boss has to know what's really involved in the job and say 'thank you' when it is done well. In doing that they show they appreciate something very important.

This is it.

Often, something that looks like a really big deal is actually quite easy to achieve. Something that looks small, however, can be heroic.

People close to the work always know the difference. Bosses who applaud the wrong things cause more damage than bosses who don't congratulate at all.

Recognition that celebrates real merit, not luck, powers smart and successful businesses.

Confident, successful businesses know when it's right to say 'thank you' and when to do it, too.

Say sorry

Wine Bar Theory businesses are polite. Because they know it makes a difference.

They say 'thank you', good morning', 'please' and, whenever it's called for, they apologize.

Whether it's with customers, suppliers or a member of the team, when smart businesses make a mistake they recognize it as a critical moment. You can either build a lifetime of loyalty or lose the relationship altogether. It just depends how you respond.

Great businesses show their human face when there is a problem. They show they care and they put things right, fast.

My bank account ran into unauthorized overdraft when I was a student. The bank manager, nearing retirement, called and asked me if I planned to get a job one day and when I said I did he signed the overdraft off with no charge. I kept the account for the next 25 years.

Whenever a customer has reason to complain, smart businesses respond fully, not grudgingly. They apologize for falling short, they write to the customer personally, explain why it won't happen again and send a gift or voucher to say 'thank you' for showing them where they went wrong.

Why does it matter?

This is why.

A retrieved customer becomes an advocate for your business to others. An aggrieved customer tells everyone not to deal with you. They both dine out on your story.

Smart businesses recognize the importance of saying sorry and tackling issues head on. They should never be surprised by how people react. If they are, they have only themselves to blame.

Businesses that are surprised by people's responses to the things they do have failed to do a very simple thing. It's the next rule.

"Your most unhappy customers are your greatest source of learning."

BILL GATES (1955–)
CO-FOUNDER OF MICROSOFT
AND PHILANTHROPIST

(27)
Stand in the other person's shoes

It's odd how rarely, when a problem or a conflict arises, people in business think to ask how they would feel about it themselves if they were personally involved. It's almost as if they don't believe their own human reaction is relevant.

But it really is.

Whether your problem is with a customer, a colleague or the person who delivers the sandwiches, ask yourself how you would like to be treated if you were them.

Try asking these questions in the mirror:

How would I feel if I was in their situation?

What would I do if it was me?

Would I accept that?

Would I think it was fair?

"Life's most insistent and urgent question is what are you doing for others?"

MARTIN LUTHER KING (1929–68)
CLERGYMAN AND
CIVIL RIGHTS LEADER

How would I expect it to be resolved?

Then make sure your business gives the answers you would hope for yourself.

Remember the third rule of Wine Bar Theory?

Keep asking.

Asking simple questions, and thinking how you would feel in the other person's position, helps resolve conflict.

It's easier to solve other people's problems than our own. Everyone knows exactly how things should be done, because they know their boss could get so much more out of them if only they knew how to relate to people better.

So when you face a problem in business, go stand in the other person's shoes first and see how it feels. Then respond.

Simple really.

Wine Bar Theory holds that it is best to find the most efficient and effective way of doing business so you can spend more time in the wine bar.

Proponents of Wine Bar Theory believe in working smart, not long. That doesn't make them shirkers. It makes them thinkers.

They say 'thank you' and 'sorry' at the right times, put themselves in others' shoes and lead by example. They know big must not mean slow. They know to give responsibility to the right number of the right kinds of people. They know how to stand things up bravely, because they don't guess answers and they invest in things that work. They know to be careful what they cut, because it's growth that matters and the right costs make things that make their customers rich as well as them. They know why they are different, where they're heading and why they have to keep asking simple questions. Because they want to keep going.

When people go to a wine bar, they enjoy themselves. They motivate, inspire, entertain and encourage each other. It's a positive place. The place you work should not be so different. Just without the wine, perhaps. Except when you're celebrating.

If you follow the 28 Wine Bar Theory rules that should be quite often.

28? Yes, sorry. One more ...

"Time you enjoy wasting is not wasted time."

JOHN LENNON (1940–80)
MUSICIAN, SINGER AND SONGWRITER

Enjoy!

It's allowed and it really helps. People enjoy working in brilliant businesses. That's one of the things that makes them brilliant.

So go make it happen.

Now you know how.

'I light my candle from their torches'
Robert Burton (1577–1640), scholar

Across my 35 years in business, and before, there have been countless
people to whom I owe a deep debt of gratitude and who in many and
different ways have taught me important things which have contributed
to the writing of this book. If I tried to list them all it would double the size
of the book and offend Wine Bar Theory too. So my special thanks to:
Vivien Ainley, Philip Brown, Bill Butcher, Victoria Clarke, Henry Cooke,
David Davies, Danielle Donougher, Don Gilbertson, Jocelyn Gilbertson,
Susanna Kempe, Patrice Klein, Iain Lindsay-Smith, Laura Nickoll,
John Quilter, Amanda Renshaw, Peter Rigby, Trevor Tarring, Vanessa
Todd-Holmes, Stuart Wallis, Maurice Watkins – and all the others.

David Gilbertson

Phaidon Press Limited
Regent's Wharf
All Saints Street
London N1 9PA

Phaidon Press Inc.
180 Varick Street
New York, NY 10014

www.phaidon.com

First published 2013
© 2013 Phaidon Press Limited

ISBN 978 0 7148 6583 6

A CIP catalogue record for this book is available from the British Library.

Illustrations by Bill Butcher
Designed by Edwin van Gelder at Mainstudio

Printed in China